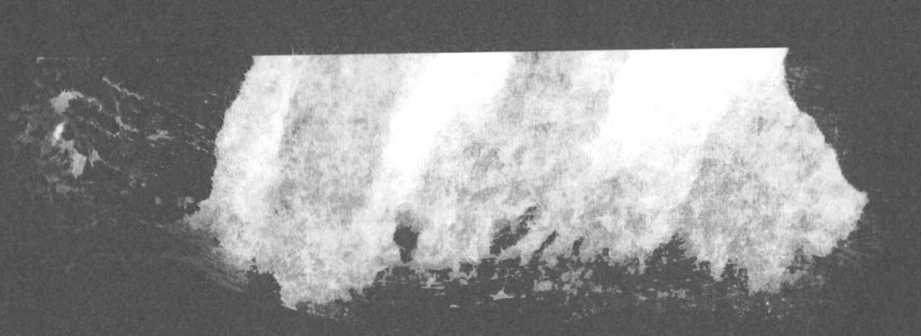

Victorian Britain

VICTORIAN HEALTH

Fiona Macdonald

FRANKLIN WATTS
LONDON•SYDNEY

First published in 2009
by Franklin Watts

Franklin Watts
338 Euston Road
London NW1 3BH

Franklin Watts Australia
Level 17/207 Kent Street
Sydney, NSW 2000

Dewey classification number: 614.409

ISBN 978 0 7496 8678 9

Planning and production by Discovery Books Limited
Editor: Helen Dwyer
Design: Simon Borrough

Printed in China

Franklin Watts is a division of Hachette Children's Books,
an Hachette UK company.
www.hachette.co.uk

Photo credits:
Discovery Picture Library: pp. 4, 10, 11, 13, 24, 25 top, 25 bottom (Bobby Humphrey); George Marshall Medical Museum (Catriona Smellie): pp.16, 17, 21, 22; Peter Hepplewhite: pp. 5, 9; Mary Evans Picture Library: pp. 8, 12, 14, 15, 18, 19, 23, 27; The Old Operating Theatre Museum and Herb Garret: p. 20 both; www.picturethepast.org.uk: p. 6 (Courtesy of Derby City Council); Museum of the Royal Pharmaceutical Society, GB: pp. 6, 7, 28, 29.

Contents

When Victoria Became Queen

Early Victorian Britain had fast-growing industry, the latest technology and some of the world's leading engineers, inventors and scientists. Its population was increasing dramatically and its cities were expanding rapidly.

Short lives

In spite of these impressive developments, Britain at the start of Queen Victoria's reign was not a healthy place to live. In 1832, a doctor in Leeds wrote: 'Not 10 per cent of the inhabitants of large towns enjoy full health.' Government statistics of births, marriages and deaths – recorded from 1837 onwards – support his opinion. They show that a child born to a working-class family in a crowded British city in the 1830s might expect to live for only 29 years. In contrast, a child born to a wealthy family in the countryside might live for at least twice as long as a city child.

Then and Now: Causes of Death

Victorian people died young from illnesses and injuries that can mostly be cured or prevented today. The chief causes of death were **infectious diseases**. Accidents at work killed many men, and childbirth was dangerous for women. Many people were underfed or **anaemic**.

Today, most people in Britain die of diseases that come with old age, such as heart attacks, strokes and cancer.

Dirty, dangerous working conditions killed many Victorians. These children are working underground in a coal mine. The air is polluted and they have no safety equipment or protective clothing.

This Victorian tombstone records children from one family who died aged two, one, eight (in a railway accident) and four.

Tuberculosis

One of the deadliest diseases in Victorian times was **tuberculosis** (TB). People at the time called it the 'White Plague' or 'Consumption'. One British doctor estimated that it killed one in four people while they were still young. Its symptoms included coughing, fevers and spitting blood. Most victims grew very thin and pale as the disease 'consumed' their health and strength. It spread especially fast among poorly fed, overtired workers in dirty, crowded towns.

Pain and suffering

If we could travel back in time to 1837, we would see people suffering from chronic (long-lasting) diseases that weakened and exhausted them; pain for which there was little relief; incurable infectious diseases that killed them frighteningly quickly; and injuries or **inherited** conditions that disabled them permanently. They would also have been fearful for themselves and their families, and grieving for the many people who died young.

This book will look at some of the reasons for the short, sickly lives of many Victorian people, and at how doctors, nurses, scientists and campaigners tried to improve the nation's health.

Doctors and Quacks

In the 19th century, there was no free health care. Patients had to pay for doctors, medicines, nursing care and hospital treatment. Many people could not afford doctors' fees and were looked after by their families at home. Hospitals were often run by charities. They were dirty and dangerous, so patients were terrified to go there. Nurses were untrained, unreliable, sometimes dirty and often drunk.

Body Snatchers

So many young men wanted to become doctors that universities and medical schools could not find enough bodies for them to study. According to the law, only executed criminals could be **dissected**. So grave robbers dug freshly buried bodies from tombs and sold them to doctors. In 1829, all Britain was scandalised when two labourers, William Burke and William Hare, were found guilty of murdering around 30 poor people in Edinburgh, to sell their bodies for dissection.

A Victorian ***pharmacist*** *with jars and bottles of medicines in his shop. Many of these medicines were helpful, but some were useless. Others were dangerous if they were used wrongly.*

Physicians, surgeons and apothecaries

Although doctors charged high fees, many were unqualified. In 1837, there were three different kinds of doctors. Physicians treated patients with medicines and fashionable cures such as hydrotherapy (hot baths, cold showers and drinking lots of water). They were the

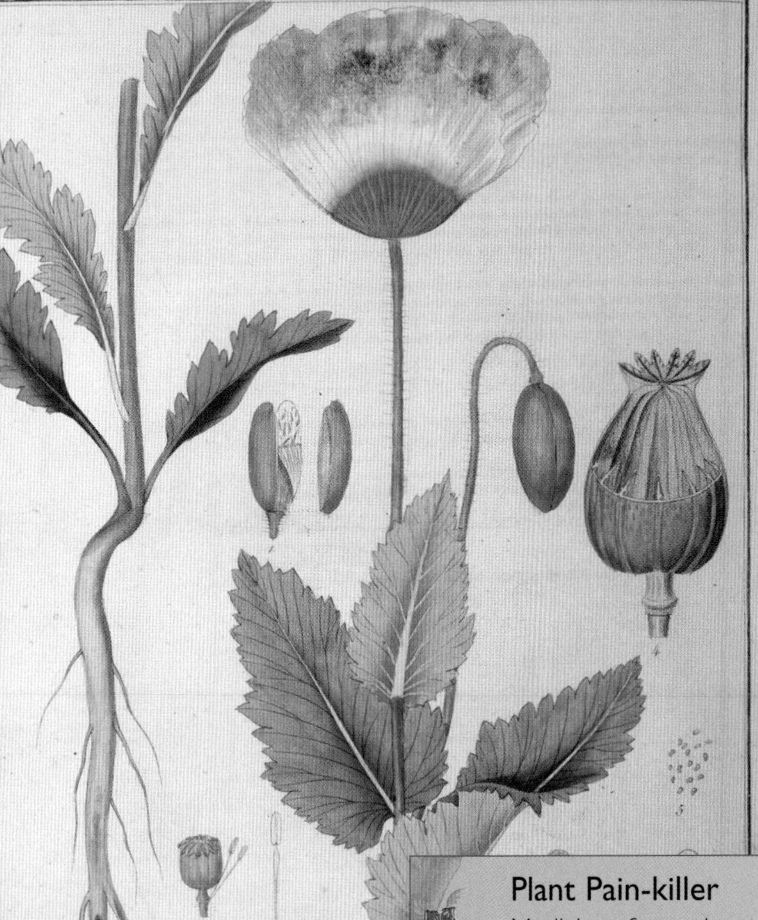

best-trained doctors. Most had attended university to study **anatomy**, but they still did not know how many body parts worked or that blood, bones and flesh were made of microscopic **cells** with different functions.

Surgeons pulled teeth, set broken bones and performed operations. They learned through watching and helping senior surgeons at work or by going to medical school.

Apothecaries were local, low-ranking doctors who bandaged wounds, supplied simple medicines and suggested basic home treatments such as bed-rest and soft food. They trained by attending lectures and working in a hospital for just six months.

Medical alternatives

There were also a few physicians who used alternative treatments, such as **homoeopathy** (first used in 1796). There were a great many **quacks** who sold cheap, dangerous, useless pills and potions to poor people desperate for help.

Plant Pain-killer

Medicines from plants had been commonly used in Britain for centuries. Like the ancient Egyptians and the Romans before them, Victorian apothecaries and doctors relied heavily on extracts from the opium poppy (above) as pain-killers. In 1871, one doctor wrote: 'Opium is ... our chief medicine for relieving pain and procuring [bringing] sleep … the physician [doctor] could ill spare it in his battle with disease.'

Unhealthy Cities

Cities grew very fast throughout Victoria's reign. For example, the population of London was around 800,000 in 1801 but by 1901 it numbered an amazing seven million. Many other cities, although they were smaller, grew even faster.

Letter from a Poor Worker in London

*Sur … We … beseech (beg) your proteckshion and power. We live in muck and filth. We aint got no priviz (toilets), no dustbins, no drains, no water-splies, and no drain or suer (**sewer**) in the hole place … The Stenche (stink) of the Gulley-hole [pit for sewage] is disgustin. We all of us suffer, and numbers (many of us) are ill.*

To the editor of *The Times* newspaper, 1849.

Smoke belches from steelworks' chimneys in the busy city of Sheffield, 1884.

Polluted air

People moved from the country to work in new industries that developed in or next to cities: textile factories, metal foundries, potteries, chemical works or mines. They lived as close as they could to their workplaces, breathing air that was polluted by factory smoke, coal dust or poisonous fumes.

Overcrowded housing

Working families crowded together into small, cheaply-built rows of houses or tall tenement (apartment) buildings. These had no running water or toilets and few windows to let in fresh air. They were damp, mouldy and infested with disease-carrying insects, such as cockroaches that fed on rotten food and bed-bugs that

When houses had no toilets, city families used outdoor privies as shown here filled with ash from coal fires. These had to be emptied once a week.

sucked human blood. Often, whole families shared one room. All the people in an apartment block or row of houses had to share just one outdoor cold-water pump and one outside lavatory.

Polluted food and water

The water from the shared pumps was often dangerously polluted by factory waste and human sewage. Rubbish was heaped up in back courtyards or on street corners. Gutters were stinking and filthy.

Many foodstuffs had to be transported long distances from country farms to feed the city people. On the journey, foods began to go bad or were contaminated by dirty rats, mice and flies. To make more money, shopkeepers often added dangerous substances to food, such as mixing dirty water into milk, sand into sugar and sawdust into flour.

Many poor working people simply could not afford enough food. Going short of food meant that children did not grow properly. Many were weak and stunted (abnormally short) or had **rickets**.

NO HELP FOR THE POOR

Some doctors, scientists, politicians, and other wealthier people saw how poor workers suffered. They were also worried by the cost of helping poor, sick people. So Parliament asked a civil servant, Edwin Chadwick (1800–1890), to investigate.

Chadwick's report

In 1842, Chadwick published a 'Report on the Sanitary Conditions of the Labouring Population'. In it, he said, that the 'loss of life from filth and bad ventilation [polluted air] is greater than the loss from death or wounds in any war'. He called on city councils to build drains, move rubbish from the streets, improve water supplies and employ city medical officers.

These homes in Leeds were built for workers in Victorian times. Whole families lived in single rooms.

It was the first time that anyone had spoken in public about the link between poor living conditions and health. Chadwick also claimed that it would be cheaper to clean up towns and improve housing than to go on giving help to the poor. He said that if people stayed healthy, they would be able to work and support themselves. In 1848, Parliament passed a law setting up a Board of Health, encouraging city councils to take the actions that Chadwick had recommended.

Councils take no action

Most city leaders ignored the law. This was partly because reforms were expensive, and rich citizens did not want to pay higher local taxes; partly because they did not like being told what to do by Parliament; partly because they blamed 'wicked' or 'lazy' working people for their own sickness and poverty; and partly because they did not understand how dirt caused disease.

Oppositon to Chadwick

We prefer to take our chance ... than be bullied into health. Everywhere the board's inspectors were bullying, insulting and expensive. They entered houses and factories insisting on changes revolting to the habits or pride of the masters or occupants. There is nothing so much a man hates as being cleaned against his will, or having his floors swept, his walls whitewashed, his pet dung-heaps cleared away.

Part of an article in *The Times* newspaper, 1854, criticising the Board of Health set up by Parliament in 1848 following Edwin Chadwick's report.

One of the worst jobs in the world! This man earned a living by hunting through sewage for lost property. He was probably not aware that he risked catching serious diseases from the sewage.

Cholera Epidemics

Many dangerous illnesses spread rapidly among poor workers in crowded, unhealthy towns. Typhus (carried by lice), typhoid (found in dirty food) and tuberculosis (passed on by coughing and spitting) killed hundreds of thousands. Then in 1831, a deadly new epidemic disease called cholera arrived in Britain.

Agony and panic

Cholera brought panic and fear. Its symptoms were violent cramps and uncontrollable vomiting and diarrhoea. Infected people collapsed, turned ghastly pale, and died, in agony, within hours. No-one knew what caused it, and no doctor could cure it. There were more cholera epidemics in 1848 and 1854. So many people died, and so fast, that some said it was the end of the world.

Studying the epidemic

One London doctor, named John Snow (1813–1858), stayed calm and began to study the 1854 outbreak. His researches focused on the area around Broad Street, a crowded part of London where 500 people had died in less than 10 days. He noticed that most of the

A cartoon published in 1858 showing 'Father Thames' (a dirty river, right) bringing his 'children' (deadly diseases) to the city of London.

CHOLERA.

THE

DUDLEY BOARD OF HEALTH,

HEREBY GIVE NOTICE, THAT IN CONSEQUENCE OF THE

Church-yards at Dudley

Being so full, no one who has died of the CHOLERA will be permitted to be buried after *SUNDAY* next, (To-morrow) in either of the Burial Grounds of *St. Thomas's*, or *St. Edmund's*, in this Town.

All Persons who die from CHOLERA, must for the future be buried in the Church-yard at Netherton.

BOARD of HEALTH, DUDLEY.

Orders for burying cholera victims. So many people died, so quickly, that new graveyards had to be found for them.

people killed by cholera took their drinking water from one particular pump. Strangely, workers in a nearby brewery stayed healthy, even though they mixed with other local people in the neighbourhood streets and shops. The brewery workers never drank Broad Street pump water. Instead, they preferred the brewery's own private water supply or its beer.

Polluted water

Snow realised that cholera must have been spread by water from the Broad Street pump. In 1854, most cities and towns had no proper sewers. Snow discovered that a **cesspit** next to the Broad Street pump was cracked and leaking. Sewage from the cracked cesspit was polluting the pump's water. Snow disabled the Broad Street pump and the Broad Street cholera outbreak ended. He had proved that cholera was spread by polluted water.

The Miasma Theory

Before John Snow's researches most Victorians believed that contagion (breath or smells from sick people) or miasma (bad air from boggy ground or dirty water) caused disease. The worse the miasma smelled, the more dangerous it was. They thought that miasma somehow weakened healthy bodies and caused fevers.

THE GREAT STINK AND AFTER

In the hot, dry summer of 1858, London's citizens were faced by a new health problem. Water levels fell in the rivers and streams that supplied London's drinking water, causing what became known as 'the Great Stink'.

In particular, the River Thames, which flows through the capital city, was much lower than usual and much more smelly. There was not enough water flowing along to carry away all the sewage and other rubbish that Londoners regularly poured into it.

New sewers

The smell from the half dried-up River Thames was so bad that Members of Parliament (MPs) were forced to stay away from the Houses of Parliament, which were right beside the river. They ordered immediate improvements to London's drains and water supply. A leading engineer, Joseph Bazalgette (1819–1891), was asked to rebuild London's sewers.

Joseph Bazalgette

Building a sewer system in London was an enormous task, but Joseph Bazalgette completed it splendidly. Between 1859 and 1885, his men built 134 kilometres of huge, brick-lined sewer tunnels leading into the River Thames far downstream from London. These were linked to 1800 kilometres of smaller sewers under London's streets and houses. They are still in use today.

Deepening the sewer along Fleet Street in the heart of the city of London, in 1845.

The Great Clean-Up

In 1867, many more working men in towns and cities gained the right to vote. They wanted to live in cleaner, healthier cities and Parliament had to take their demands seriously.

In 1875, with the support of opposition Liberal MPs, Parliament passed the first of several laws that became known as 'the Great Clean-Up'. The 1875 Public Health Act said that city councils had to employ medical officers (public health doctors) and sanitary (hygiene) inspectors. They were also told to provide drains, sewers and public toilets for their citizens. Public baths and wash-houses began to be built, so that the poorer classes could enjoy a greater level of hygeine.

In 1876, more laws were passed. They laid down improved standards for all workers' housing; gave local councils the power to clear away **slums**; started regular rubbish collections; banned food contamination; and tried to stop river pollution. Soap became much cheaper, and healthier food was provided for people in towns.

The public baths and wash-house in Newcastle upon Tyne, which opened in 1859.

Medical Science and New Technology

From around 1870, British people's health also improved because of new scientific discoveries made in other parts of Europe.

Exchanging ideas

All through the 19th century, British doctors and scientists read reports in European journals about the latest medical discoveries and new techniques for surgery. They also sent notes of their own discoveries to share with European colleagues. Doctors from Britain and Europe also travelled to study and teach at each other's medical schools and universities. In the same way, British doctors passed on their findings to doctors and scientists in the USA and visited America to study what was happening there.

Looking inside the body

New, sensitive stethoscopes, which helped doctors listen to the heart and lungs, were invented in 1816 in France. An improved stethoscope that transmitted sound to both ears was developed in the USA in the 1850s. The ophthalmoscope, to examine the inner eye, was created in 1851, and a machine to look down the throat into the stomach appeared in 1868.

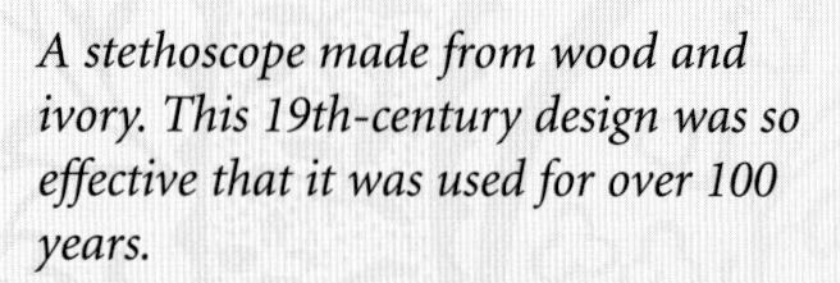

A stethoscope made from wood and ivory. This 19th-century design was so effective that it was used for over 100 years.

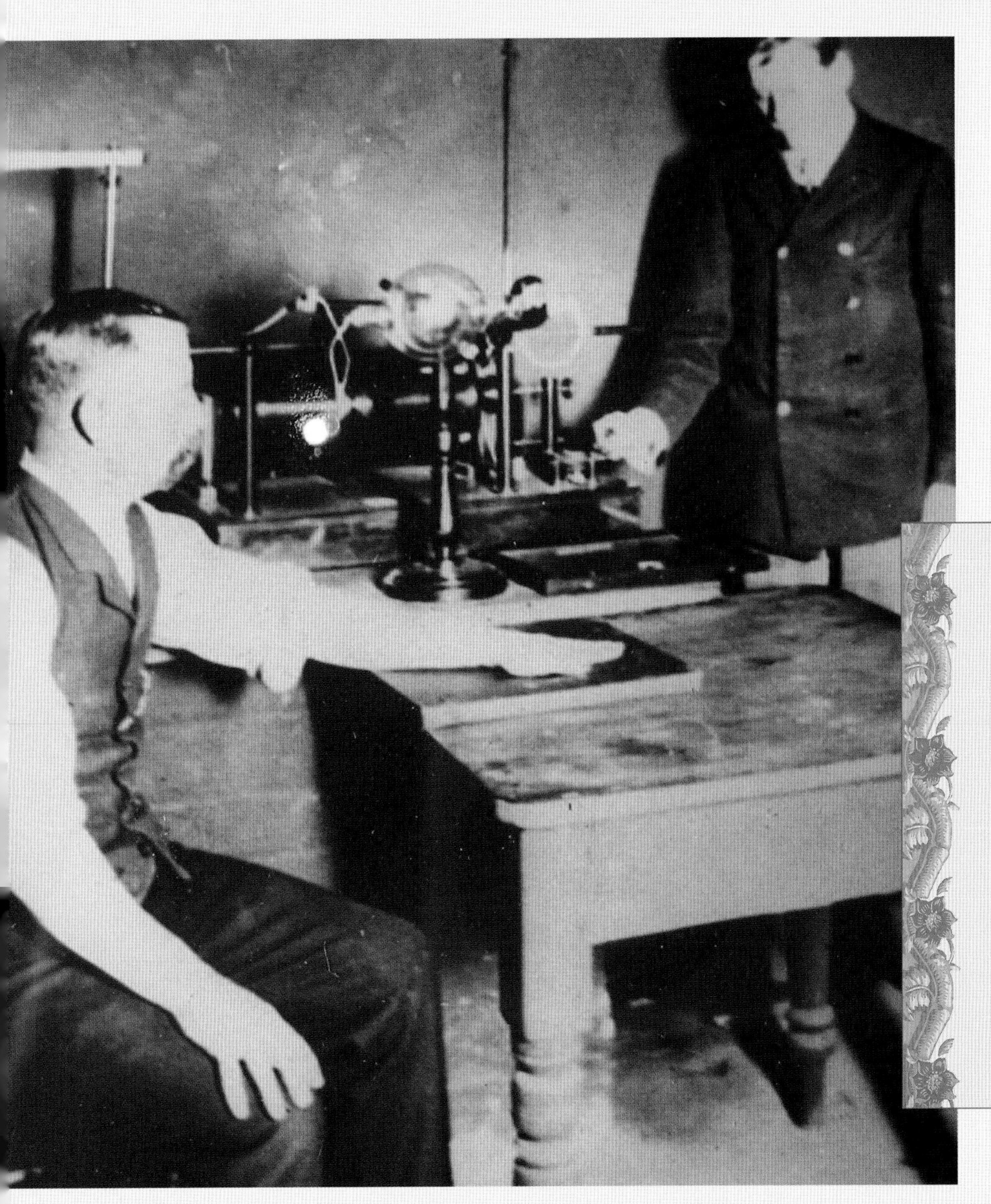

Victorian new technology. One of the first X-ray machines in Britain, at Castle Street Infirmary, Worcester.

X-rays

The most exciting new way of investigating the body – X-rays – was discovered by German scientist Wilhelm Conrad Röntgen (1845–1923) in 1895. For the first time ever, doctors could see inside living people to examine broken bones and dangerous 'foreign bodies' such as bullets.

Simple hygiene

The first great European medical breakthrough came in 1847, when Hungarian doctor Ignaz Semmelweis (1818–1865) ordered his medical students to wash their hands before examining women giving birth in hospital in Vienna, Austria. Semmelweis felt sure that the students, who had been cutting up dead bodies, were carrying germs straight from the corpses to the mothers and their babies. As the students obeyed his orders, the death rate fell from 29 mothers in each hundred to only three per hundred.

Like John Snow and cholera in London, Semmelweis had discovered how disease spread and had stopped it but without being able to explain why. Soon however, discoveries in France would provide a solution to that mystery.

UNDER THE MICROSCOPE

French experimenter Louis Pasteur (1822–1895) was a scientist, not a doctor, but he was keenly interested in the causes of disease. He began work in industry, as a chemist, and, in 1854, he took on a new project. His task was to find out what was causing huge flasks of juice, being used to make alcohol, to **ferment**.

Microscopic organisms

Using the latest microscopes, Pasteur had examined samples of fresh juice and compared them with juice that had fermented. He found that the fermented juice was full of tiny micro-organisms. Today, we would call them yeasts or bacteria. He also found that putting these micro-organisms in milk and wine made liquids go sour. Pasteur proved that the bacteria came from the air. He felt sure that the micro-organisms in soil, water and many other environments might cause diseases in humans and animals.

Louis Pasteur in his laboratory looks through a microscope on his desk. Microscopes improved during Victorian times, allowing scientists to identify different bacteria.

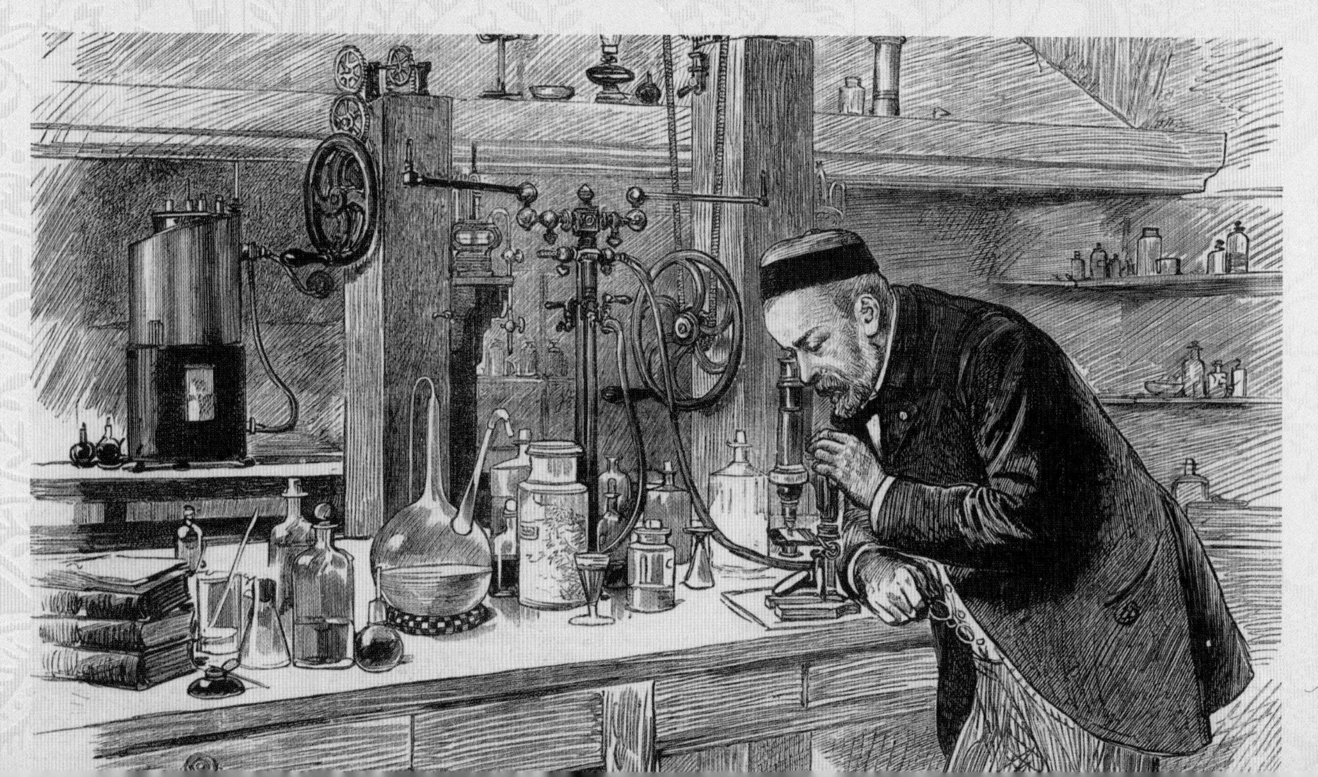

Identifying bacteria

At the same time, German scientist Robert Koch (1843–1910) was also making exciting discoveries. He invented ways of studying bacteria in sealed, clean glass panels (microscope slides) so that they did not become mixed with other organisms from the air. This helped him make a great discovery. In 1876, he realised that each different disease was caused by a different organism. Koch identified many new kinds of bacteria and also found ways of growing them in laboratories, to study. In the 1880s, he made more major discoveries: the bacteria that caused the diseases tuberculosis and cholera.

Matching blood

One of the greatest dangers after surgery, accidents and childbirth was loss of blood. Many attempts to **transfuse** some blood from a healthy person had failed, and no-one understood why. Then in 1900, Austrian Karl Landsteiner (1868–1943) discovered that red blood cells contain substances called **antigens** which clump together dangerously when mixed with antigens that are different. Landsteiner recognised four different human blood groups: A, B, O and AB. Each group had a different pattern of antigens. If sick people were given blood with antigens that matched their own, it would save their lives, but blood with different antigens would kill them.

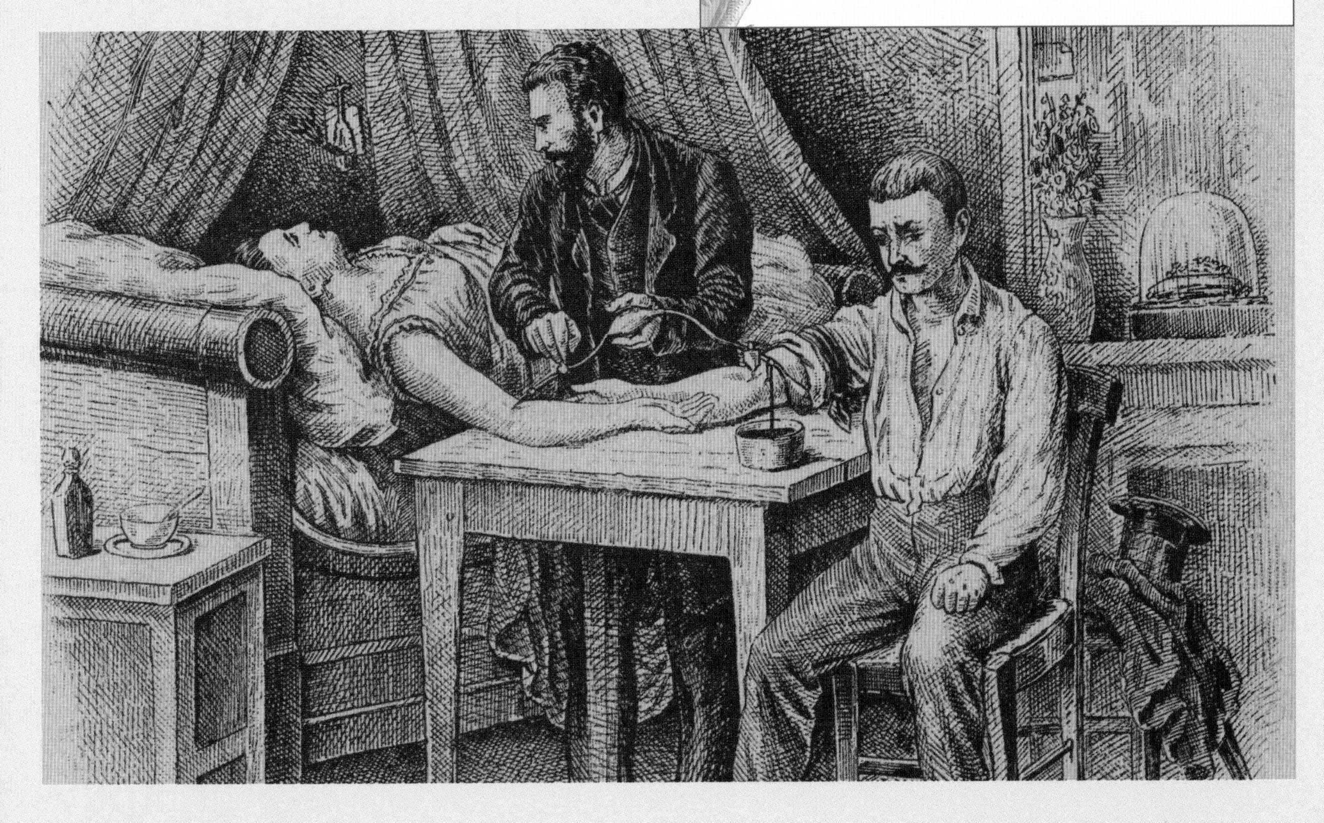

A blood transfusion, 1880. A husband is giving blood to his wife. No-one knows whether it will save her life or kill her.

Relief from Pain

Meanwhile, back in Britain, doctors were searching for ways to reduce pain during operations. Pain relief was also needed by women in childbirth, for dental treatments and for patients dying of certain incurable diseases.

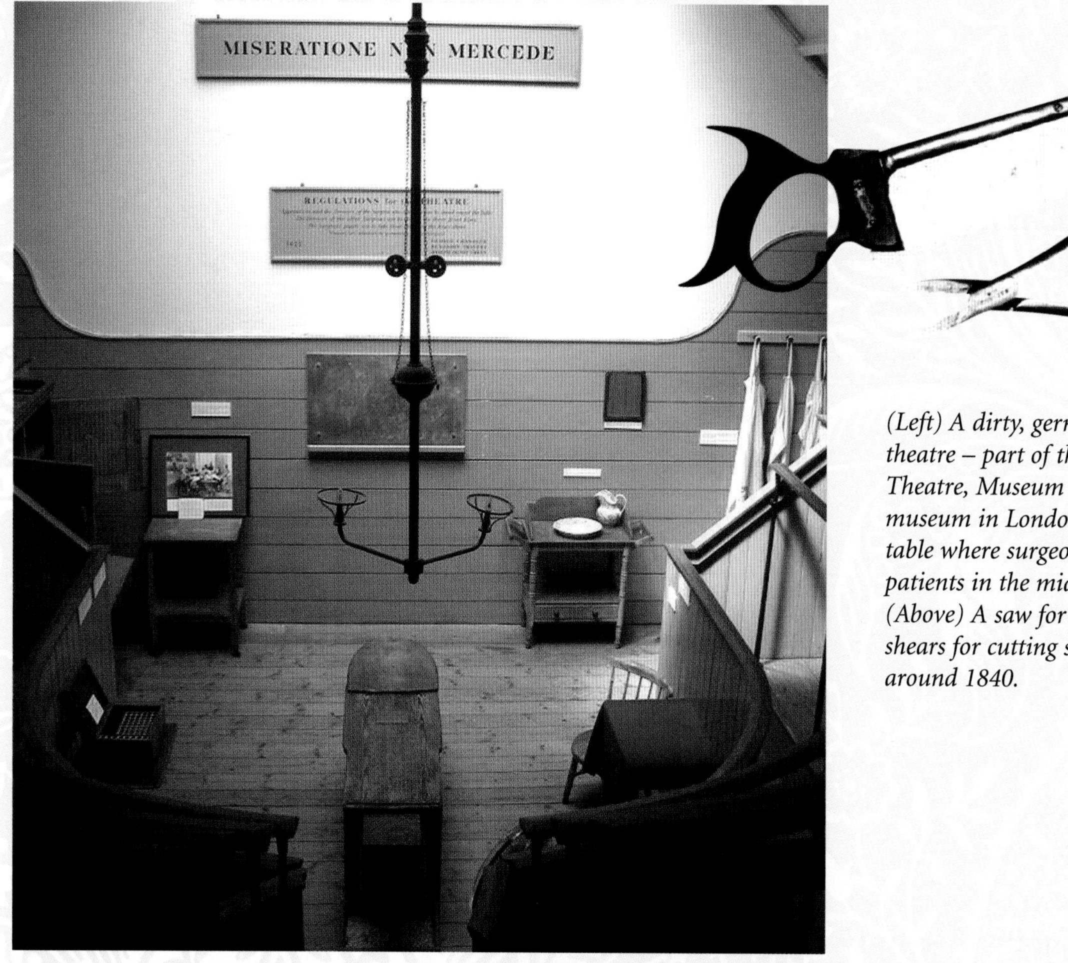

(Left) A dirty, germ-filled operating theatre – part of the Old Operating Theatre, Museum & Herb Garret museum in London. You can see the table where surgeons worked on their patients in the middle of the room. (Above) A saw for cutting bones, and shears for cutting skin and flesh, from around 1840.

The agony of surgery

At the start of Victoria's reign, patients remained wide awake during surgery. Their faces might be covered by a handkerchief, but they could still hear what was happening. The shock of such extreme pain killed some patients. Others died from loss of blood, but most were killed by infections.

To lessen the pain as much as possible, the best surgeons worked very fast, cutting off an arm or a leg in just one or two minutes. Drugs were sometimes used to make patients unconscious, but they were so dangerous that many people never woke up again! A new, safe, **anaesthetic** was badly needed to prevent the pain of operations.

Pain as Punishment

Chloroform quickly became fashionable, although not everyone approved of it. Some medical and religious leaders condemned it. They said that pain and suffering were God's punishment for sin and that pain relief was unnatural.

Laughing gas

Since the late 1700s, scientists had known that a gas called nitrous oxide made people light-headed; another gas, ether, had a similar effect. In the USA, both were used in fairground sideshows. Customers paid for a few whiffs of 'laughing gas' for entertainment. Between 1842 and 1846, American dentists and doctors anaesthetised the first patients with nitrous oxide and ether to pull out teeth and perform simple operations. In 1846, the first British operation with ether anaesthetic took place.

Chloroform

Next day, the newspaper headlines proclaimed 'We have conquered pain!' The truth was not quite so simple. Like many other powerful drugs, nitrous oxide and ether both had damaging side-effects. They were soon replaced by another gas, **chloroform**. In 1853, doctors gave chloroform to Queen Victoria, to ease pain during the birth of her seventh child. The queen was delighted, saying that the anaesthetic was 'soothing and quieting'.

Chloroform is a liquid that evaporates very quickly, producing anaesthetic gas that patients can breathe.

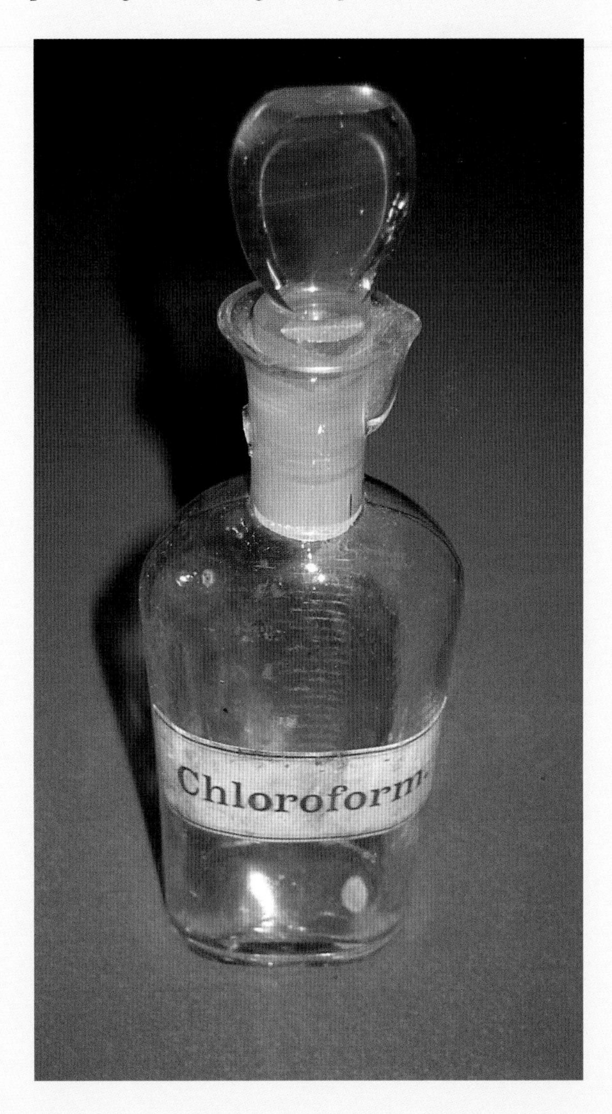

ANTISEPTICS

With their patients drowsy and pain free, surgeons dared to perform new, complicated and risky operations. As more and more operations were performed, more and more patients died, mostly from infections caused by bacteria – from the air, walls, floors, unwashed knives, blankets and dressings, from doctors' clothes (surgeons did not change before operations), and from doctors', nurses' and students' hands.

Carbolic acid

A senior surgeon, Joseph Lister (1827–1912), knew that carbolic acid, a powerful **antiseptic**, was used to kill germs in sewage. So, in 1865, he experimented by treating a badly wounded boy with dressings soaked in carbolic acid. To almost everyone's surprise, the boy survived.

Vapouriser for making carbolic acid mist, used to disinfect operating rooms around 1870.

Soon after, Lister began to spray the room where he operated – and all the people in it – with a mist of carbolic acid. He also made doctors and nurses wash their hands in carbolic acid mixed with water. Lister's records show that, before he used carbolic, almost 46 out of every 100 of his patients who had an amputation (arm or leg cut off) died from infection. Once he began to use carbolic spray, this total fell to only 15 patients out of every 100.

Cleaning and sterilising

Lister's methods were copied and improved by doctors elsewhere in Europe and the USA. Doctors used steam to sterilise operating rooms, knives and other surgical instruments. Surgeons and nurses began to wear thin rubber gloves, face-masks, and fresh, clean gowns for each operation. By 1890, Lister and other British doctors stopped using carbolic spray and slowly adopted these new techniques. Operations were now much safer.

The Power of Carbolic Acid

A boy aged 11 years was admitted to Glasgow Infirmary on 2 August 1865 with a compound [serious, cut-open] fracture of the left leg caused by the wheel of an empty cart passing over the limb a little below the middle.

A piece of lint dipped in carbolic acid was laid over the wound, and splints padded with cotton wool were applied. It was left undisturbed for four days and, when examined, it showed no sign of suppuration [oozing with infection].

At the end of six weeks, I found the bones united [joined up again], and I discarded [threw away] the splints. The sore [wound] was entirely healed.

Report by Joseph Lister on the first case he treated with carbolic acid.

Doctors and nurses wearing clean white gowns and aprons, Charing Cross Hospital, London, 1900. Surgical masks and gloves later became essential wear in the operating theatre.

HEALTH CARE REFORMS

At the start of Victoria's reign, there was no organised system of training doctors, and almost no training for nurses. Hospitals, dispensaries (chemists) and asylums were mostly run by charities, but conditions in many were grim and dirty.

Elizabeth Garrett Anderson

Until 1876, women could not legally go to university or medical school. But Elizabeth Garrett Anderson (1836–1917) broke this rule to become the first British woman doctor in 1865. She went to hospital lectures, then fought a court case to join the Society of Apothecaries as a junior doctor. She studied medicine at university in France, then returned to London to set up a surgery for private women patients, a clinic for working-class women, and a school to train more women to become doctors.

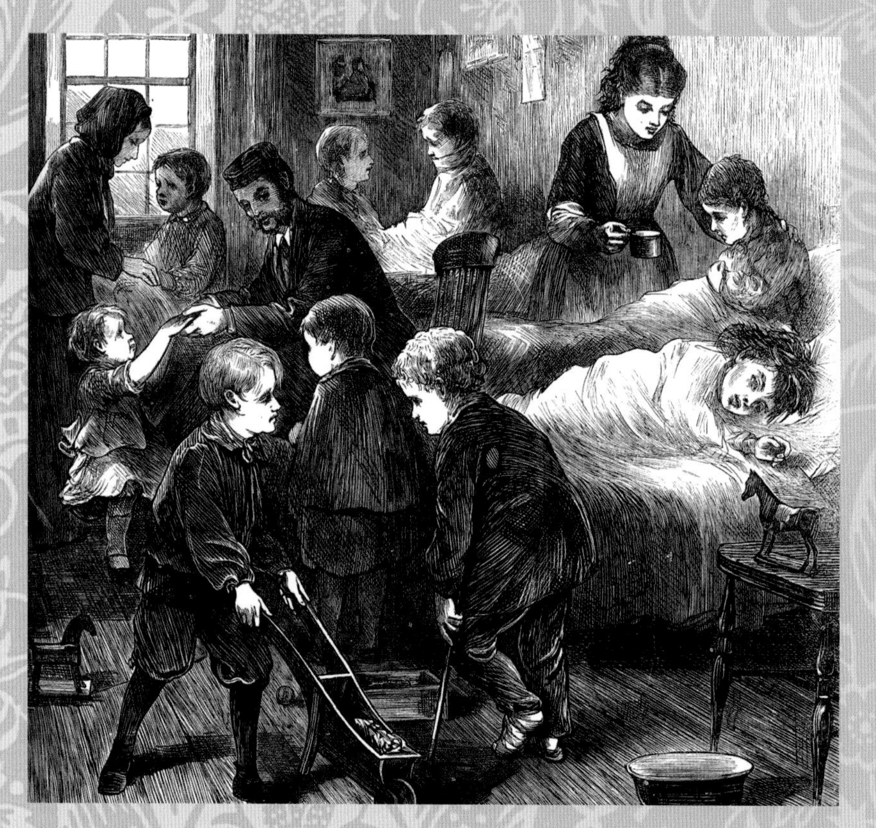

A scene from a very busy and crowded children's hospital in Stepney, London, in 1872. This hospital was run by a caring surgeon and his nurse wife, who also set up a women's clinic.

The government acts

Politicians, doctors and campaigning individuals worked hard to improve medical education, stop untrained people treating patients, provide training for nurses and raise standards in hospitals and asylums. The most important of these health reforms came in 1858, when the General Medical Council was set up, to supervise the work of physicians, surgeons and apothecaries and maintain the Medical Register – a list of properly-trained and qualified doctors. Other important reforms included local council inspection of asylums (1845), care for sick people in **workhouses** (1861), council hospitals for workers (1866 and

Medical students doing scientific experiments as part of their new, improved training, St Thomas's Hospital, London, 1886.

1867), medical officers to oversee health care (1872), registration of dentists (1880) and care for mentally less able people (1886).

Better nursing

Nursing was revolutionised by one of the most respected Victorian women – Florence Nightingale (1820–1910). In 1859, she published a book, *Notes on Hospitals* – attacking dirty, badly run wards – and a training manual, *Notes on Nursing*. In 1860 she set up the first British nursing school at St Thomas's Hospital, London. She taught nurses to observe their patients scientifically and keep careful records. Above all, she insisted that hospitals should be very, very clean.

Nightingale's method's worked. Hospitals were transformed. Deaths rates in the worst dropped from 40 per cent to just 2 per cent. By 1888, the new British Nurses' Association had more than a thousand fully-trained members.

The Royal Infirmary, Leeds, was built following new rules for hygienic hospitals made by Florence Nightingale. It had light, bright, airy wards with plenty of bathrooms and lavatories.

In the Mind

Victorian people did not know what caused mental illness or the mental problems that people were born with. However, they had many theories to explain these conditions.

Conflicting theories

Many doctors believed that mental problems were caused by families 'degenerating' (decaying in stages) from one geneneration to the next. For example, the grandparents might have been anxious; their children – the parents – might then take drugs; the parents' children might be 'insane' (with unbalanced minds) as a result; and the children's children might be idiots (completely unable to think). Other doctors said that people with mental illness were an earlier, less developed, type of human being, with low, heavy brows and jutting jaws, like apes.

County asylums

Parliament passed an act in 1845 which made it compulsory for every county to have an asylum for mentally ill people. Proper records had to be kept and doctors had to be employed.

People in asylums faced a life of strict discipline and hard work, such as washing the laundry and chopping firewood. If they were unable to work

The Derby County Lunatic Asylum, opened in 1851. It had room for over 300 patients, kept in by a brick wall nearly 1.6 km long.

E. Mackenzie delt

J. H. Le Keux sc.

A room in Broadmoor criminal asylum, Devon. It housed law breakers with serious mental illnesses, such as artist Richard Dadd (1817–1886). He killed his father – and painted very strange pictures of fairies.

they had to march around yards for exercise. The wards were locked and there were railings around the buildings to stop anyone escaping.

Attempted cures

Some doctors believed that mental troubles had a physical cause and could be cured by surgery. Others tried to reform patients' characters, often by cruel shock treatments, such as burning them, spinning them around for a long time or throwing them into barrels of slimy, squirming live eels.

A few doctors tried gentler treatments, such as setting up communities where patients lived in family groups supported by carers. Then, in 1899, Austrian doctor Sigmund Freud (1856–1939) published a new theory: mental illness was caused by disturbances in 'the unconscious mind'.

Freud's New Ideas

Sigmund Freud was the first doctor to suggest that the human mind works unconsciously (without us knowing) as well as consciously (by thinking and learning). He believed that all our actions were guided by our unconscious mind as well as by conscious thoughts and feelings. He tried to understand the unconscious by studying dreams, fears and memories. He also thought that forgotten childhood experiences might cause mental illness much later, in adult life.

Health at the End of Victoria's reign

Queen Victoria's reign saw many new discoveries and developments in medicine and health care. By 1901, when Victoria died, the causes of killer infections were understood. The search was on to find medicines that would kill the newly discovered germs that caused illnesses such as tuberculosis.

New understanding

Scientists understood much more about how the body was made and how its different cells functioned. Doctors could use new technology, such as X-rays, to diagnose disease. Doctors and nurses were much better trained, and new professional organisations controlled the way they worked. Hospitals were cleaner, safer and well-run. The treatment of people with mental problems was slowly becoming kinder and more understanding.

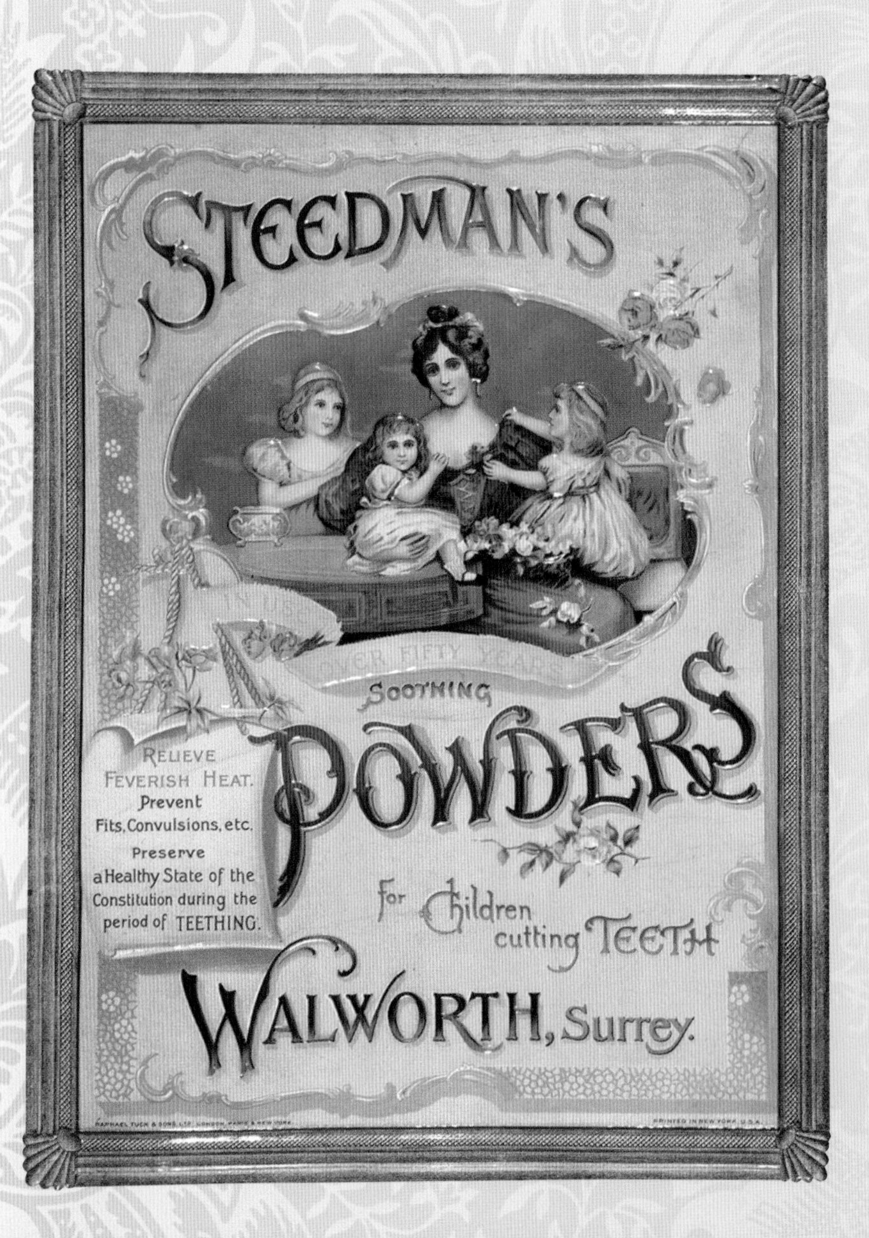

Late Victorian medicines could still be very dangerous. These powders to soothe teething babies contained morphine (heroin)!

This handsome chemist's shop, photographed around 1900, displays 'cures' of all kinds. Even at the end of Victoria's reign, poor people still could not afford them.

A healthier environment

National and local governments now understood that they had a duty to provide healthy environments for their citizens. New sewers and piped water made cities cleaner; new laws tried to control pollution, remove rubbish, improve housing, supply safer food and provide emergency hospital care.

Unsolved problems

In spite of all these improvements, problems remained: patients had to pay for medical care, and it was often very expensive; there were not enough trained doctors and nurses; and many public health services were organised by local councils, so some places were much healthier to live in than others.

Most important of all, many people in Britain in 1901 were still very poor. They could not afford good food and lived in dirty, slum streets and the worst, most unhealthy, houses. This made them the most likely group to fall ill and need medical treatment, but they were also among the people unable to pay for it.

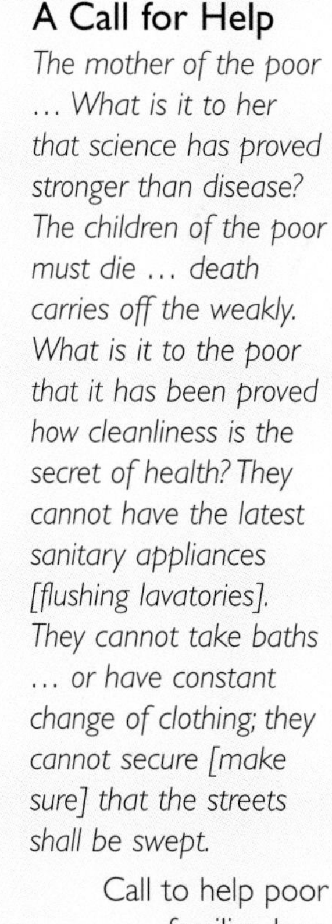

A Call for Help

The mother of the poor … What is it to her that science has proved stronger than disease? The children of the poor must die … death carries off the weakly. What is it to the poor that it has been proved how cleanliness is the secret of health? They cannot have the latest sanitary appliances [flushing lavatories]. They cannot take baths … or have constant change of clothing; they cannot secure [make sure] that the streets shall be swept.

Call to help poor families, by a clergyman, 1889.

Glossary

anaemic lack of blood or of red blood cells.

anaesthetic a drug to dull the senses.

anatomy the study of the structure of bodies.

antigen a substance foreign to the body.

antiseptic a substance that stops the spread of bacteria in the body.

asylum a home for large numbers of mentally ill people.

cells microscopic units of living material that work independently or with other cells in animals and plants.

cesspit a pit for the waste from shared lavatories.

cholera an epidemic disease that was spread through contaminated water supplies.

chloroform a poisonous liquid containing chlorine, used to dull the senses.

civil servant an administrator who works for the government.

dissected cut up into pieces for scientific examination.

epidemic an infectious disease that is easily passed from person to person and affects many people at the same time.

ferment become sour and fizzy as chemicals break down.

homoeopathy a system of alternative medicine using minute doses of substances that would cause the symptoms they are treating if they were used in large doses.

infectious diseases diseases that can be passed from one person to another.

inherited received from parents or more distant ancestors.

pharmacist someone who prepares and sells medical drugs.

quacks medical cheats and frauds.

rickets soft and deformed bones, caused by a shortage of vitamin D.

sewers pipes or tunnels made to take away human waste.

slum housing unfit for human habitation.

transfuse transfer blood from one person to another.

tuberculosis a serious, often fatal lung disease.

typhoid a disease with diarrhoea and vomiting.

typhus a disease carried by lice.

vaccination injecting micro-organisms to produce artificial resistance to disease.

workhouse an unpleasant refuge where the very poor had to live if they had no money.

Timeline

1837 Victoria becomes queen.
1842 Edwin Chadwick publishes a report on the conditions of workers.
1845 Every county must have an asylum for the mentally ill.
1846 First British operation with ether anaesthetic.
1847 First use of chloroform as an anaesthetic.
1848 Cholera epidemic; Boards of Health set up in the cities.
1854 Cholera epidemic; John Snow discovers that cholera is spread by polluted water.
1858 General Medical Council is set up.
1859 Work on the London sewer system begins.
1860 Florence Nightingale sets up first British nursing school in London.
1865 Joseph Lister uses carbolic acid to kill germs; Elizabeth Garrett Anderson becomes the first British woman doctor.
1875 Councils must provide clean water, drainage, sewage disposal and medical inspectors.
1876 Robert Koch discovers that specific bacteria cause diseases.
1895 X-rays discovered.
1900 Blood groups identified.
1901 Queen Victoria dies.

Places to Visit

Florence Nightingale Museum, London
http://www.florence-nightingale.co.uk/cms
The museum tells the story of the life and work of Florence Nightingale, the founder of modern nursing in Britain.

George Marshall Medical Museum, Worcester
http://www.medicalmuseum.org.uk
The museum houses a collection of objects illustrating the way that medicine and health care has developed over the past 250 years.

Old Operating Theatre, Museum and Herb Garret, London
http://www.thegarret.org.uk/index.htm
The only surviving 19th-century operating theatre, with table and observation stands. The museum displays include a collection of surgical instruments and specimens, and exhibitions tell the story of local hospitals and herbal medicine.

Thackray Museum, Leeds
www.thackraymuseum.org
Tells the story of medicine and explains medical advances. Experience the living conditions in early Victorian Leeds, find out about medicine and surgery then and the progress made in medicine since.

Websites

http://www.bbc.co.uk/history/british/victorians/victorian_medicine_02.shtmlV
An article on the Victorians section of the BBC website entitled: 'Victorian Medicine – From Fluke to Theory'.

http://www.medicalmuseum.org.uk
The website of the George Marshall Medical Museum in Worcester. You can click on medical equipment through the ages and find out what it was used for; diagnose the illnesses of children in Worcester in 1861 from their symptoms and read about their home lives and diets; and perform a leg amputation on screen and learn about the dangers of surgery.

http://www.thackraymuseum.org
The website of the Thackray Museum in Leeds has two Interactive games: comparing surgery in 1840 and today; and looking at the work of Victorian nurse Mary Seacole.

http://www.learningcurve.gov.uk/victorianbritain/healthy/default.htm
From the National Archives. This website provides primary resources such as documents and historical pictures for you to decide whether Victorian Britain was a healthy nation.

http://www.channel4.com/history/microsites/H/history/guide19/part06.html
Channel 4 Time Traveller's Guide to Victorian Britain microsite. Section on 'Hazards & Dangers'.

INDEX